GIFTS *of the* SPIRITUAL WILDERNESS

- A LENTEN DEVOTIONAL -

J. DANA TRENT

chalice
press

Saint Louis, Missouri

An imprint of Christian Board of Publication

For Mary June: Tusen Tack.

Bible quotations, unless otherwise noted, are from the *New Revised Standard Version Bible,* copyright 1989, Division of Christian Education of the National Council of the Churches of Christ in the United States of America. Used by permission. All rights reserved.

Cover design: 99 designs

Print: 9780827212930   EPUB: 9780827212947
EPDF: 9780827212954

ChalicePress.com

Printed in the United States of America

Table of Contents

Introduction

Dear Readers

We tend to think of "wilderness" as a dry, thirsty place. The word "wild" itself conjures up an unpredictable habitat in which humans are especially vulnerable. But Christ reminds us that what, on the surface, may seem dangerous, uninhabitable, and deserted—is a land of plenty.

We are no strangers to places of drought. The world's grit has left us parched. Years of communal and individual loss, grief, violence, injustice, oppression, and unrest have made us exhausted. We are no strangers to the wasteland. But what does this unruly, scarce, and wild landscape teach us about faith, spirituality, and the Triune God? How does Jesus' forty days in the wilderness intersect with our own twenty-first–century experiences? This Lent, you are invited into daily exploration: discerning the unlikely gifts of our discomfort.

Consider These Questions for Your Journey:

- What does Jesus's biblical retreat into solitude, sacrifice, and spiritual practice teach us about the gifts of our modern wilderness experience?
- How might a spiritual drought actually create a more meaningful Lent experience?
- What do fasting, sacrifice, and temptation look like in our contemporary daily lives?
- How might we prepare our bodies, minds, and spirits to experience new life—and gifts—on the other side of this Lenten journey?

Through daily devotions with scripture, meditations, practices, prayers, and "living water" tools for our parched lives, this Lenten guide is a companion for a contemplative and transformational journey from the wilderness to resurrection.

Your Invitation: Chalice Press and I encourage you—beseech you—to be open to the spiritual gifts of the wilderness, including drought lessons that bear fruit all year long. This little book is your fellow traveler: Place it near your favorite Bible, journal, or scratch pad. Set a time that suits you to complete each day's reading. Take some deep breaths. Reflect earnestly. Sit with any discomfort—and surprises—as you move through the deserted places to Easter communion.

Scripture References and Themes: This book uses the *New Revised Standard Version's* Old and New Testament to center our reflections and

1

enrich your journey. But feel free to use whatever version you have on hand. As we move through Lenten days and weeks, you are invited to consider these themes deeply: facing spiritual droughts, taking inventory of our parched lives, sacrifice and spiritual practice, walking through the wilderness to get to living water, living water for our parched lives, and gifts of the spiritual wilderness. When you encounter a scripture, reflection, or question that loosens a difficult emotion, allow it to bubble up. Take it one breath at a time. This guide is an honest, sincere, and empathetic real-talk book about discovering the gifts of comfort in the uncomfortable—like a well-stocked backpack that will not leave you empty and alone. We are on the path together—and I brought snacks.

Spiritual Practices: Each day contains a one-minute journal prompt and a prayer. As the weeks progress, the journal prompt will be woven with additional spiritual practices of meditation (breathing and silence) as well as the Ignatian Examen (noticing). Practice the art of "progress, not perfection" with these tools: Journal imperfectly, meditate poorly, and pray clumsily. Spiritual practices are a launch pad for receiving God's gifts.

Finally, I must confess: The wilderness makes me itchy. I don't like literal or metaphorical dirt and dust. And I'd certainly rather not shake out grit from the cracks, crevices, and folds I didn't even know existed. But I also know, symbolically, that the gift of bright blue living water I love so much is nearly always surrounded by rough topography and textures. I know that I cannot get to the heart of the matter—the restorative waters—without trekking the sand. We cannot arrive at Easter resurrection without wilderness wrestling.

On this journey with you,

J. Dana Trent, April 2021

Prayer: *Loving God, guide our sandy feet and our weary way. Equip us to turn inward and face the dreaded drought in order to discover the spiritual abundance. Amen.*

Dust and Ashes

Job 42:6

*"Therefore I despise myself,
and repent in dust and ashes."*

My friend the chaplain quotes this line from Job each time she makes a mistake. Tiny or large, in jest or deliberate, she offers this earnest and biblical confession of transgression. When we discuss her Job reference, she reminds me that no one says "sorry" like Job.

On Ash Wednesday each year, we are called to humility and apologies. But most of us dread a day of *teshuvah,* re-turning toward things we'd rather not be reminded that we thought of, said, or did. We'd prefer not to face what needs mending because we're already ashamed. We'd prefer not to face death, because we already feel the pinch of time. But these reminders—that our actions matter and our bodies are finite—are a good start to discovering the spiritual gifts of Lent.

As we experience the real smudge of ashes on our foreheads, we are invited into a metaphorical place of Job-ness. We need not endure Job's exact suffering to embrace Ash Wednesday as an opportunity: an inciting incident that invites us to authentic spiritual struggle and its subsequent gifts. This year, I invite us to exchange Ash Wednesday drudgery for eager expectation.

Spiritual Practice, One-Minute Journal: Make two columns. In one column, list all the things you dread about Lent. In the other, list all the things that make you eager for this liturgical season—even if small. Pay attention to both columns. From there, craft an intentional statement of what you'd like to glean from these first days of Lent.

Prayer: *God who hears our confession, help us to wear these ashes with humility, starting the journey as beginners who have a lot to learn from the wilderness and knowing that you are with us every step of the way. Amen.*

Immediacy

Mark 1:1–13

And the Spirit immediately drove him out into the wilderness. (v. 12)

After his baptism, Jesus *immediately* retreats to a deserted place for spiritual boot camp. Most of us, after our baptisms, were celebrated with family photos and luncheons.

But the gospel of Mark is *urgent*. It's jam-packed with verbs; the word "immediately" (*euthys* in Greek) occurs forty-one times. Mark is also the first gospel written, so it comes out of the gate running, throwing its readers and Jesus into the thick of it. There is no slow-going, no post-baptism luncheon, no midday nap. There is *immediacy*.

In the same way, we are invited into the wilderness with gusto. It's no coincidence that Christ's baptism is followed by a forty-day physical drought to induce spiritual plenty. If Jesus is our model, we are asked to practice the same essence: diving into Lent with full force.

I've always found it interesting that Jesus' ministry begins with his human vulnerability. Before a word was taught, a sermon preached, a person healed, a miracle produced—Christ is driven by the Spirit to the wild. Grit, solitude, isolation, sacrifice, temptation—these are the *first* and *immediate* practices after the lush, living water of the River Jordan. From the safety of John, friends, and family, Jesus goes to the deserted place to distill the essence of what is to come.

Christ's forty days in the wilderness is our exemplar: If we are going to get to the root of faith, we must strip bare the things of this world that keep us tethered. Instead of avoiding, evading, and running, we are invited to *immediately* dive into the wild spaces and recalibrate to our ultimate purpose: faith.

Spiritual Practice, One-Minute Journal: Make a list of what's holding you back from the *immediacy* of the Lenten wilderness.

Prayer: *Triune God, lift our hesitations and debunk our excuses. May your Spirit drive us into this bountiful season immediately. Amen.*

More Questions than Answers

Psalm 13:1–6

How long, O Lᴏʀᴅ? (v. 1)

Zora Neale Hurston, author of *Their Eyes Were Watching God*, reminds us that, "There are years that ask questions and years that answer."[1]

In real life, we've just begun to wrestle with deep questions. We began a decade (2020) with an unexpected and terrifying pandemic, catastrophic death, fear, violence, and unrest. We asked, "Why, God?" and "How long, O Lord?" over and over. Looking back, it's no surprise that this heart-wrenching period began during the season of Lent, which, at the time, seemed unusually cruel. But in the rearview mirror, it's appropriate: Lent is about asking the *hard* questions; it's a journey of spiritual inquiry to distill what really matters.

The good-bad news is that during the pandemic, we remained in a sort of perpetual Lent. We were forced to examine the most awful parts of our collective and individual humanity—the gritty, uncomfortable, sandy parts of ourselves that needed to be shaken from complacency. The pandemic ripped the curtains down and showed us the service and work that needed to be done. It made us tune in to the questions that mattered, so that we could inch toward the answers we needed. Seems like a metaphor for the wilderness journey, no?

The post–2020 temptation might be to skip all future Lents, pat ourselves on the back, and say, "We lived all the questions already and now we have all the answers." But that is not the practice. That is not the call of Christianity. When we stumble into the unknown again, how do we press our palms together in supplication and admit we don't have the answers?

Spiritual Practice, One-Minute Journal: Write down life's biggest questions for you *right now*. Don't overthink it. Write the questions that come to mind first, with little concern for the answers.

Prayer: *Holy One, help us to sit with the discomfort of uncertainty and inquiry. Remind us that we don't need to know all the answers in order to be kept and comforted by your grace. Amen.*

---

[1] Zora Neale Hurston, Their Eyes Were Watching God (Champaign, IL: University of Illinois Press, 1991), 27.

Bread of Life

Matthew 4:1–11

"'One does not live by bread alone,
but by every word that comes from the mouth of God.'" (v. 4)

Who doesn't love bread? It's nourishment that fills us from our nose to our toes. Scripture can do the same, but so often, we don't think of it that way. Biblical texts have been historically misused to harm and oppress others. Sometimes we don't consider it nourishment but, rather, baggage.

Because this book is a companion for dipping in, navigating, and gleaning fruit from unexpected places—such as the wilderness—I invite us to do the same with Bible verses. To seek the essence of these texts as bread—without the dread. Jesus was no stranger to the complexities of sacred texts. But he didn't off-load them; he saw them as integral to his faith—and life.

If we've been poor Biblical students lately (I have), how might these wilderness accounts—and all scripture we'll explore this Lent—help us unwrap unexpected gifts of nourishment?

Bring on the bread basket.

Spiritual Practice, One-Minute Journal: Reflect on the ways in which scripture has both challenged you and invigorated you. In what ways has the Bible been your "bread of life"?

Prayer: *Holy One, you feed us in many ways. Help us to be open to the ways in which these sacred texts fill our empty bellies and hungry souls. Amen.*

Week 1:
Facing Spiritual Droughts

Challenge Accepted

James 1:2–3

Because you know that the testing of your faith produces endurance. (v. 3)

My pastor, Marcus, loves the book of James. He tells remarkable stories about his mentor who claimed that James, in fact, is the quintessential guide to Christianity. But we don't hear much from James in our pulpits. Why?

Because James is a tough read in a spiritual drought. It's a come-to-Jesus meeting in the wilderness about the essence of Christianity: what it is, and what it is not. Like the silence of deserted places, the book of James can be a loud reminder of how far off the mark we can be when it comes to living peacefully and mercifully, being civil and loving.

We often balk at taking a close examination of our internal lives, especially in times of spiritual drought. When things feel hopeless, it's hard to have authentic James-ish conversations about *real* faith, spirituality, right, and wrong. Even during flourishing times, that level of discernment is painful. We'd much rather enjoy the dopamine rush of the external: entertainment and avoidance. Our human bodies and brains are designed to steer clear of conflict, testing, and challenges, to keep us safe. If it's not pleasant, let's not discuss it. But James says that the fruit is found in the discomfort.

Times of testing—such as the devastation of a pandemic, the sacrifice of a year of isolation, or any other collective human grief and catastrophe—cannot be without higher meaning and purpose. Although we do not diminish the pain of suffering, we do ourselves a disservice not to notice its fruit: lessons in loving deeply, serving faithfully, and turning inwardly. The gifts of austerity are real. It's a matter of finding them.

The best news? The Bible is a candid companion for this journey. Like James, these verses unwrap gifts if we are willing to sit with them even when they feel prickly or challenging.

Spiritual Practice, One-Minute Journal: How, when, and where have you been tested spiritually? Examine a time when you felt spiritual struggle. Reflect and make a list of the Lenten fruits of testing that we might remember all year long, including how physical, mental, and spiritual struggles equip us to go deeper. Consider how an authentic Lent invites us inward for deep contemplation and *spiritual* preparation for Easter.

Prayer: *God of creation, we know there is fruit everywhere. Open our eyes and help us to look for it. Amen.*

Letting Go of What Doesn't Work

John 15:2

"He removes every branch in me that bears no fruit."

Our nonagenarian neighbor is an exquisite gardener. She bends and pulls, lifts, and moves shrubs and dirt like a force of nature. Each season, she leans over the fence and encourages us to prune our roses.

"Trim, trim, trim, cut, cut, cut." she reminds us. We are reluctant pruners. My husband and I are afraid to cut back the roses or snip the azaleas for fear of killing the plants. But our neighbor is always right: When we cut the branches more than we think we should, the plant thanks us in kind; it channels the sun and water to yield gorgeous new growth and steadier-than-ever flowers.

The good-bad news is that we've been in perpetual pruning mode to understand what needs to be cut: habits, routines, and relationships that drain nutrients from our roots. The "Great Pruner" encourages us to examine the dried up, dead parts of ourselves and our communities that no longer bear fruit. Scripture teaches us to release that which keeps us weighed down. As soon as we allow God to help us let go of what is no longer serving us, we emerge from the winter seasons stronger, greener, and lusher.

Spiritual Practice, One-Minute Journal: What needs trimming in your life? What have previous or current spiritual droughts revealed about branches that are dead? What is God trying to show you that needs trimming?

Prayer: *Creator God, you are the Divine Pruner of branches that do not bear fruit. Help us to let go of the dry, dead branches that do not produce the fruit of the Spirit. Amen.*

Spiritual Season

Ecclesiastes 3:1

For everything there is a season, and a time for every matter under heaven.

The longer I live, the more I love the book of Ecclesiastes. It's full to the brim with wisdom, including the cyclical, seasonal nature of the human journey. I'm now well into my fourth decade, and I've yet to experience a tougher season than a global pandemic. It has been the ultimate spiritual drought: a wasteland of death, grief, loss, despair, uncertainty, isolation, stress, anxiety, and weariness.

But there has been something about this season—a time for every matter under heaven—that has awakened and stirred us. We had been going, doing, buying, and moving at a 24/7 pace for decades, thinking ourselves invincible and our time and connections infinite. We took for granted hugs, touch, health, safety, sabbath worship, and gathered community.

Amid its devastation, this pandemic "season" jolted us from complacency, just as the writer of Ecclesiastes was stirred from the ordinary to realize that change is the only constant.

When we realize this cyclical nature of humanity and faith—that spiritual plenty and drought come in waves—we are more likely to stay present in the moment, taking it for precisely what it is: a season.

> **Spiritual Practice, One-Minute Journal:** Describe the "season" of your life right now. Using imagery and embodied language, show your experience and journey just as it is.

Prayer: *God of time, we know that you accompany us in every season of life: from drought to abundance, from peace to unrest. You are the ever-steady constant, and we are grateful. Amen.*

Ego is the Enemy

Ecclesiastes 1:2

Vanity of vanities, says the Teacher,
vanity of vanities! All is vanity.

Even fervent Lent enthusiasts face the annual discomfort of a wilderness experience. Wilderness, after all, assumes drought: a climate lacking in lush greenery. Wilderness is a landscape seemingly void of life—though not always. And biblically, wilderness signifies a place of austerity and facing the hardest parts of being human.

Jesus' time in the desert was one of sacrifice and temptation, not indulgence and egoism. Like Jesus, we face conceptual and metaphorical adversaries, forces that encompass the spaghetti strands of human experiences that induce suffering: vanity, selfishness, pride, vices, ego, and all the spiritual deserts that lead us to oppress ourselves and others. The gospels write of Jesus' retreat to the deserted place as a period of self-exile for spiritual and physical refinement. Jesus' wilderness narrative includes temptations that encompass the most basic human hang-ups, to show us how spiritual drought can make us especially susceptible to costly missteps. In other words, the physical and mental wilderness is not an easy place to be.

Our Sunday school teachers taught us that although Jesus was tempted by vanity, power, and material goods, he stood his ground, and we should, too. The things of this world: ego, authority, possessions—all fall away with time. What endures, even amid the harsh environment and austerities, is the spiritual fruit from the drought. And for Jesus, the fruit had infinite impact: a vibrant, three-year ministry that changed the world.

Spiritual Practice, One-Minute Journal: Make a quick list of the aspects of your life and ego where you are *most* vulnerable to give in to temptation. No judgment, just sincerity.

Prayer: *Holy One, you have shown us how to cope with the pressures of being human through the life and experiences of Christ. Equip us to be more Christ-like in our ego-effacement and detachment from things of this world, so that we may dive deeper into our relationship with you. Amen.*

Virtues and Vices

Luke 4:1–13

Where for forty days he was tempted by the devil. He ate nothing at all during those days, and when they were over, he was famished. (v. 2)

In *Summa Theologica*, thirteenth-century theologian Saint Thomas Aquinas helps readers frame Greek virtues in a theological context. Prudence, justice, temperance, courage, faith, hope, and charity—these are the characteristics we seek to embody as disciples of Christ. But in what seems counterintuitive, these virtues are cultivated best when life isn't easy. As an example, it's far easier to be courageous when we are not confronted by a circumstance in which we are called to be brave.

Jesus, as our model, is tempted by the adversary when in his most vulnerable state: he's alone, isolated, famished, and weak. It is then that Satan (which literally translates from Hebrew as "adversary") begins a series of tests. In lieu of giving in to his hunger, Jesus remains steadfast in his prudence, justice, temperance, courage, faith, hope, and charity at a time when it would have been much easier to cave. If Jesus' adversary—and our adversaries—tempted us with food after we've had a full meal, how tempting is that? Not very.

Jesus is tempted during a physical drought; we are often tempted during our spiritual ones. With Christ as our model, we know that God comforts us in our hour of temptation. And as we read the final of the three gospel accounts of the wilderness (Mark 1:1–13, Matthew 4:1–11, and Luke 4:1–13) we are reminded just how difficult Jesus' forty-day journey was.

Spiritual Practice, One-Minute Journal: Recall a time when you stood up to an adversary and did the right thing—and how it felt.

Prayer: *God of humanity, we know that we are your fragile and beloved creation. We are capable of virtues and vices, and you have given us free will to choose each day. May we look to Christ's example. Amen.*

Vices and Virtues

Proverbs 20:9

Who can say, "I have made my heart clean;
I am pure from my sin"?

Vices stand in contrast to virtues. They are the behaviors, moods, and states of being, mind, and body that we turn and re-turn to when we are not living into the fullness for which we were created. From lust to gluttony, greed, sloth, wrath, envy, and pride—not one of us traveling this Lent is perfect. We have encountered each of these vices at some point our lives—metaphorically and literally, in times of both spiritual flourishing *and* drought. What matters is how we recognize our vices, cope with them, and inch toward virtue.

"Sins" and "vices" are not easy to examine, to be sure. But part of the Lenten invitation is to look at the most hidden, difficult, shameful parts of ourselves. When we do, we are free to do the work of spiritual pruning: cutting through the dry, dirty, dusty, dead parts of ourselves to discover the spiritual gifts—and fruit.

Spiritual Practice, One-Minute Journal: Make a private list of the vices, sins, or obstacles you are encountering this Lent. Do not be hard on yourself. This is not a call to judgment. Rather, this is a self-examination for the sake of growth. Allow that which troubles you to bubble up on the page so you can face it with God's help.

Prayer: *Holy God, it's easy for us to forget we are beloved to you, no matter what. Our vices and sins do not keep us from being truly, deeply beloved in your eyes. Help us to remember that this eternal, unconditional love comes only from you. Our willingness to let go of what keeps us tethered to the "adversaries" of our lives helps us to draw nearer to you. Amen.*

Beloved

Lamentations 3:22

The steadfast love of the LORD never ceases,
his mercies never come to an end.

The most important part of any wilderness journey is knowing that we are loved. Before the Spirit drove Jesus out into the wilderness, Christ was baptized by John the Baptist. And when Jesus rose out of the waters, God said: "This is my Son, the Beloved."

Beloved. Be loved. Before Jesus began his aesthetic practices, his fasting, and his wilderness spiritual testing, he was loved. Loved. God's love for Jesus was made known in the accounts of his baptism.

We can endure the spiritual droughts and the weary wilderness if we know we are loved. Before we move into Week 2, where we are invited to examine ourselves and take inventory of our parched lives, we are invited to sit with God's love. As you journal today, I invite you to imagine beams of holy light shining on your face and God reminding you that no matter the wilderness, no matter the adversary, no matter the vice—you are beloved. Be loved.

Spiritual Practice, One-Minute Journal: Make a list of all the things God loves about you. Go on. Don't be bashful; you are beloved.

Prayer: *Loving God, so often we neglect to remember that we are loved unabashedly by you. As we seek to turn within for a deeper examination, may we make this love our compass's true North—the direction by which we navigate our Lenten journey. Amen.*

Week 2: Taking Inventory of Our Parched Lives

12TH DAY OF LENT (SUNDAY)

Searching Myself

Psalm 139:1–24

Search me, O God, and know my heart;
test me and know my thoughts. (v. 23)

Why is the wilderness a good place for facing spiritual droughts? Why is it an appropriate climate for searching? Because in the deserted places of life, something has been stripped away. Droughts indicate something has been cut off, something is *missing;* and like a real drought, we didn't realize how much we relied on water until it was gone.

In physical and spiritual droughts, what is missing can be the "water" of life: spiritual depth, a fulfilling relationship with God and others, and a sense that we are living a meaningful life. When we experience crisis and change—such as divorce, job loss, deaths of loved ones, illness, or distance from God, spiritual practice, and an in-person gathered community—we may feel as though we are deep in the drought. We are parched: Life is dried up and gritty, leaving us thirsty and longing for what was.

When our lives feel parched, sometimes the last thing we want to do is go inside and do the internal work of facing what's happening. We'd rather swim in the water of distractions: doing, moving, buying, and going. But the solution to the drought is not found in the tangible or material; it lies in the spiritual.

One way to move through a parched spiritual season is by taking a self-inventory. An inventory is a popular way to review the dried-up aspects of our physical, mental, emotional, and spiritual lives. It's a way to pause, breathe, and examine what needs internal investment.

As a person who thrives on busyness, I was faced with the reality of drought and inventory when I was diagnosed with a devastating chronic illness. Who was I if I was not a busy, working professional preoccupied with to-dos and the external world? My identity was tied to success and accomplishments. So, when my physical health forced me to slow down, I had to take stock and face what really matters when physical health is jeopardized.

When we have not nourished the inner garden of our relationship with the Triune God, all the dried-up aspects of our humanity come to light.

Spiritual Practice: During Week 2 of this Lenten study, you are invited to examine the spiritually dry places in your life. What parts of you, your environment, and your circumstances feel especially malnourished? It can be scary to assess this, but I encourage you to explore and face your fears and reservations about looking inward.

Prayer: *Merciful God, I am thirsty. Comfort and keep me in times of spiritual drought. Amen.*

Inventory

Malachi 3:2–3

He will purify the descendants of Levi and refine them like gold and silver, until they present offerings to the LORD in righteousness. (v. 3)

In the spiritually-based global program of Alcoholics Anonymous, step four of the twelve-step journey is to take a fearless inventory of oneself. We do not need be addicted to a substance or behavior to examine deeply. In fact, as Christians, we are invited to consider the ways we need to be refined and purified, to contemplate that which we are "addicted" to in life: success, ladder-climbing, external approval, affirmation, ego-stroking, buying, going, doing, staying just busy enough to avoid spiritual practice. These "addictions" are especially magnified—and sometimes generated––when we face spiritual drought.

Lent is an excellent opportunity to take an inventory of our parched lives. When we take stock of what is missing, needs refilling, needs adding, and needs subtracting, we inch toward the humility of refining and purification—like tarnished silverware that needs a little elbow grease.

It is only through acknowledging the grit, grime, tarnish, and piled-up stuff of our lives that we are free to encounter the cool, blue living water. We cannot swim in the bounty until we have examined ourselves.

Spiritual Practice: In this week's ongoing self-inventory, what are the parts of you that need refining? What are the especially rough portions of your heart and soul that could benefit from purification? Take an inventory. This is a no-judgment zone—you are invited into honest inquiry.

Prayer: *Loving God, you extend us grace day after day. Help us to remember that we are spiritual beings having a human experience, such that our tarnished souls need a little polish from time to time. Amen.*

Teeth Grinding

Lamentations 3:16

He has made my teeth grind on gravel,
and made me cower in ashes.

Sometimes a personal inventory feels like grinding our teeth on gravel. Like a trip the dentist's office to get a cavity filled, no one wants to subject themselves to the achy, skin-crawling pain of a drill on a sensitive tooth. So, why do it? Because, just like a neglected cavity spreads until it can only be treated with a root canal, our untreated spiritual "decay" will only worsen.

Without a review of what's not working, we cannot see what is and will work. When our lives are weighed down in the basement of human emotions—the damp, mildewy behaviors we attempt to hide—the molding foundation can ruin our whole house.

These "basement" feelings and behaviors are the ones we are embarrassed to admit. Sometimes we deny completely that we feel pride, envy, and resentment, or that we are manipulative and dishonest, or that we hold grudges and even stones to throw at anyone who does us wrong.

But this stuff is heavy. What if we laid it all down? This is what a spiritual inventory does. It explores the hard stuff and allows it to bubble up to the top for air like an ocean buoy. Because if we don't let it up and out, we are carrying suitcases of armor that damage our relationship with God, others, and ourselves—like grinding our teeth on gravel and cowering in ashes.

Spiritual Practice: Take a quick inventory of your spiritual and emotional "basement." What have you stored down there that needs a little sun? Make a quick list; don't overanalyze or judge.

Prayer: *God who understands us, equip us for the journey of going through the "old stuff" that no longer serves us. Help us to feel lighter and warmer. Amen.*

God Is Our Helper

Hebrews 13:6

So we can say with confidence,
"The Lord is my helper;
I will not be afraid.
What can anyone do to me?

Personal spiritual inventories are not easy. It takes courage and strength to walk down the scary basement stairs and see what's lurking down there. But the best news is that we are not doing it alone. Our inventories are not a solitary spiritual exercise. God is with us every step of the way.

Do you remember the accounts of Jesus' time in the wilderness? Look back to Week 1. Reread those scriptures and be reminded that Christ was never alone in his wilderness journey. God blessed his baptism; the Spirit sent him to the desert; and the angels attended to him. Even as the adversary tempted and tested him, Jesus knew that a Higher Power was at play. "What could anyone do to [him]?" Christ knew that God was his helper.

We are not alone. This doesn't excuse us from the work of facing spiritual droughts and taking inventory of our parched lives. Rather, it empowers and equips us to do it. No matter how dark the basement is, how tough the teeth-grinding feels, and how low we are in the ashes, God is always present with us. Even when God feels distant, scripture assures us repeatedly that "we can say with confidence, 'The Lord is my helper; I will not be afraid.'"

Spiritual Practice: Make a short list of all the ways in which you feel confident that God is with you during tough times. Look back to previous times of suffering and struggle and notice the ways in which God showed up in the quiet times of prayer and meditation, and perhaps in the presence of friends and family who have helped and guided you.

Prayer: *Holy God, you are our ever-present helper in time of trouble. Remind us not to be afraid and to embrace the confidence of being your children. Amen.*

Confess and Be Healed

James 5:16

Therefore confess your sins to one another, and pray for one another, so that you may be healed. The prayer of the righteous is powerful and effective.

For non-Catholic Christians, confession may be a sticky subject. Among the many flavors of Protestant denominationalism, there is no single liturgy for the confession of sin. There are myriad practices and nuances, from the definition of sin to whom, precisely, can absolve us from our sin. This is not a theological treatise on what qualifies as sin and forgiveness.

Instead, Week 2's taking inventory is about your *own* examination of what needs work in your life. These are our growth edges—areas of our lives, behaviors, thoughts, and feelings in which there is room for growth. This is not a time for self-flagellation; it's a time for honesty.

What parched parts of ourselves keep us from going deeper in our spiritual practice, our relationship with God, and our relationships with others? What dry spaces of our lives need some water and attention? What are the cracked and broken connections that need repair? Asking these questions helps us take an inventory, so that we can, in turn, confess our sin—what needs work.

When we do this, we set ourselves up for healing. When we pray about these elements of our inventory, our prayers are "powerful and effective."

Spiritual Practice: In your journal, examine your inventory from Day 13. As you recall what sins and growth edges you discovered, you are invited into a time of confession and release. As you pray the following prayer, consider a tangible way you'd like to use to mark today as a point of forgiveness from God and self-forgiveness. Light a candle. Take a walk. Sit in silence. Write a letter to yourself. Do something that sets this day apart as the day you released your inventory.

Prayer: *Loving God, we confess our sins. We confess the parched parts of our lives that keep us from living wholly loving lives. In your mercy, hear our prayer. Amen.*

Let It Go

Psalm 55:22

*Cast your burden on the LORD,
and he will sustain you;
he will never permit
the righteous to be moved.*

Sometimes our spiritual inventory can reveal significant burdens we've been carrying a long time. It takes much energy to hold unforgiveness, envy, resentment, bitterness, and lies; it takes a lot of time to chase after things in the name of greed and material gratification.

God asks us to lay down those burdens—and not pick them up again. Jesus' forty-day wilderness journey is a distillation of what really matters. Jesus doesn't bring his "stuff" to the desert. He minimizes for the internal journey. He laid down when he didn't need—and he didn't return to retrieve it. This is a hard lesson.

Like Christ, we are called to take inventory of being human in a world that parches us. We are called to lay down the burdens in order to be sustained by God. When we do, God will not allow us to falter or fail. We will be sustained by that which really matters: spiritual nourishment.

Spiritual Practice: What do you need to lay down? Make a quick list of the burdens that you need to give God. Once you have your list finished, fold your paper in half and tear it to bits. In this way, you have truly cast your burdens on the Lord and ensure that you do not pick them up again.

Prayer: *Tender God, show us that we can relinquish control. Remind us that no burden is too heavy for us to cast upon you. Amen.*

The Example of Christ

Hebrews 12:1–12

Therefore, since we are surrounded by so great a cloud of witnesses, let us also lay aside every weight and the sin that clings so closely, and let us run with perseverance the race that is set before us, looking to Jesus the pioneer and perfecter of our faith. (vv. 1–2)

It's easy to feel overwhelmed when facing spiritual droughts and taking inventory. Examining our cracked lives for dry and sinful places is probably not on anyone's spiritual wish-list. But we cannot arrive at fresh cool living water until we walk through the grit of the sand. We cannot accept the gifts of the wilderness unless we are willing to walk through it.

And the good news is that we are well-poised for this Lenten journey. We are encouraged to "look to Jesus the pioneer and perfecter of our faith." We are surrounded by a "cloud of witnesses" including Jesus and the many saints who have gone before us, who have struggled, persevered, and emerged on the other side, stronger and closer to God.

This is the hope we carry for our lives and our journey. Our faith is in Jesus. We do not need to dwell on past mistakes; we, who are weary, are called to come to Christ. And in doing so, we are invited to consider the "great cloud of witnesses" who show us how to "run the race" with perseverance. Who is your cheering section? Who are the "saints" in your life who have shown you how to go deeper in your faith?

But we can only effectively "run" (live) if we are willing to lay down the "weight" of that which we do not need: the unnecessary things—including sin—that bring us down.

I'm no runner, but I do know that it's hard to walk with extra weight on your back.

Spiritual Practice: In this last day of spiritual inventory, make a short list of everything (people, circumstances, events, memories, things) that weighs you down. Plan for how you will let one of these things go today.

Prayer: *Triune God, our steady companion on this journey, help us to lay down that which does not serve us so we can run the race set before us. Amen.*

Week 3: Sacrifice and Spiritual Practice

Why Suffering?

Romans 5:3

And not only that, but we also boast in our sufferings, knowing that suffering produces endurance.

Suffering is not a word any of us takes lightly.

The type of suffering Paul is referring to is the abstract suffering of psychological and spiritual struggle, namely the discomfort of persecution and hatred from others based on belief.

Christians who live in the United States are in the category of majority culture and religion. In this way, it's difficult to imagine persecution based on religion. Imagine though, for a moment, that you are a non-Christian being attacked for your spirituality, religion, and beliefs—persecuted for your faith. Imagine the sacrifice of comfort it would take to continue outwardly expressing your beliefs amid hostility. This is the endurance Paul wrote about. To sacrifice temporary dis-ease is a type of suffering that the apostle spoke to. In this sense, suffering does produce steadfastness and steadiness in practice. The wilderness is a place of growing and stretching our spiritual fitness. The call to follow Christ is full of sacrifice—the sacrifice of materialism, wealth, comfort, and sometimes the status quo. Consider how this kind of sacrifice leads to suffering that refines the soul.

Spiritual Practice: In this first day of sacrifice as spiritual practice, list all the ways in which you make sacrifices for your faith and religion, along with how that makes you feel. As an example, think of a time you sacrificed the comfort of fitting in in order to express your beliefs. Or, in a more tangible way, think of any time and money you may sacrifice in giving and service. If your list feels short, plan for how you may embrace additional sacrifices in the name of spirituality.

Prayer: *Divine One, help us to see that spiritual struggle is the fertile soil of spiritual growth. Amen.*

Praise and Blame Are All the Same

Job 2:7–10

"Shall we receive the good at the hand of God, and not receive the bad?" (v. 10)

Early in the book of Job, Job has a keen sense that he has been blessed by God, but also that he is not immune to suffering. In this way, Job understands that sacrifice—even temporary discomfort—is a requirement of the spiritual life. As the book of Job progresses, Job's sacrifices require more and more—from his physical health to significant loss of family, friends, and material good. These sacrifices produce suffering.

The old saying, "Praise and blame are all the same," has many different meanings, but one of the biggest take-aways is that there is a yin-yang balance to life in which one must accept the good with the not-so-good. This is the essence of what Job is saying to his wife in chapter 2. In subsequent chapters, we as readers are privy to the reality check this incites in Job. As the sacrifices cut deeper and the not-so-good becomes more prevalent than the good, we are offered a front row seat at one human's mighty wrestling with sacrifice and suffering. In the end, Job is restored because of his faith—but only after he experiences an intense season of questioning, anger, grief, physical pain, rejection, isolation, abandonment, and loneliness.

Faith is not a mountaintop-only experience. Faith is not perpetually happy-clappy; faith is not an easy path. But how do we react to God and others when things don't go our way? How do we react to God and others when life brings us suffering that we didn't anticipate? Often we are angry, frustrated, irritated, annoyed, and resentful. We are quick to blame. When our lives are disrupted, we are eager to return back to the "normal," the "status quo," which can include a life uninterrupted by suffering and sacrifice. But what if we considered that sitting with sacrifice is spiritually beneficial? Jesus is our exemplar: Christ showed us, through his wilderness experience as well as his teaching and ministry, that we are called to sacrifice.

Spiritual Practice: Recall the last time you made a significant sacrifice. Write it down and note the details. What came of that experience? What did you learn? How did you grow?

Prayer: *All-knowing God, you are present with us in the highest of highs and the lowest of lows. When we are called to sacrifice, help us to not neglect your presence and the opportunity to draw nearer to you. Amen.*

Bereft Is the Beginning of Wisdom

Lamentations 3:17

My soul is bereft of peace;
I have forgotten what happiness is.

Lament, Lent, suffering, and sacrifice are often not our go-to faith words. Bereft indicates lacking, and we do not wish for our lives to be missing something. In this way, we constantly search for and attempt to fill the void inside. We reach for stuff, substances, and people—all in a vain attempt to patch a God-sized hole.

Happiness is a tricky word. Things and experiences might make us happy for a little while. But they are temporary. We feel fleeting joy, but it's not sustainable, so we return to lacking. But what if feeling bereft is actually the beginning of wisdom and peace? What if sitting with our emptiness is truly the preparation to receive God's spiritual gifts? What if in our lacking—our stripped-down wilderness of sacrifice—we distill what's most important? It seems counterintuitive, but the more we turn inward for our happiness, the more satisfied we feel.

> **Spiritual Practice:** What does happiness mean to you? Jot down a list of things that make you happy. Examine your list. What aspects of your happiness are dependent upon material goods, things, success, people, places, and the external journey? What aspects of your happiness are dependent upon God, faith, spiritual practice, and the internal journey?

Prayer: *God, you know our hearts and our happiness. Help us to strive for that which is eternal and not fear being bereft of that which is finite. Amen.*

Chasing the Wind

Ecclesiastes 4:6

Better is a handful with quiet
than two handfuls with toil,
and a chasing after wind.

When I was in my thirties, I believed that working, going, rushing, chasing, and doing would fulfill me. "Crazy-busy" was my mantra; I worked multiple jobs and published four books in six years. I ran until I hit a wall: There was only so much doing that I could physically and mentally sustain.

I learned that all the running—the "success" of being on the go—was not fulfilling. I ended up with more toil than I wanted, chasing after that which would never satisfy me. My mother's unexpected death stopped me in my tracks.

I was forced to slow down, take deep breaths, and embrace the waves of grief. I learned that not chasing external things led to a more fulfilled life, one in which meaning-making is more important than any temporary worldly success.

Spiritual Practice: Consider the Ecclesiastes verse. Now reflect on a particularly ambitious part of your life. What were you chasing and why? Did you find happiness? What did you miss in the meantime?

Prayer: *God of quiet, nudge us to reflect on the spaces of our lives where we are chasing something in vain. Amen.*

Flesh and Bones

Job 19:20–27

*"My bones cling to my skin and to my flesh,
and I have escaped by the skin of my teeth." (v. 20)*

Often we run, chase, and do in order to avoid suffering and sacrifice. To be in spiritual, physical, mental, and emotional pain is to feel the pinch of our human finitude. By diminishing discomfort, even if temporarily, we can believe ourselves to be immortal. But Christ—in his divinity and humanity—showed us a better way.

Consider the gospel accounts of Jesus' wilderness experience we read in the beginning of this Lenten journey. Christ fasted for forty days; he was without company and comforts. In his humanity, I imagine he felt his bones clinging to his skin and to his flesh. I imagine he felt the suffering of his sacrifice. To be sure, Christ experienced temptation. He knew the pain of hunger, loneliness, fatigue, and desperation. But Jesus also knew that the experience of his desert sacrifice, spiritual practice, and reliance on God would yield dividends far more powerful than a glimpse of limited, physical comfort.

Spiritual Practice: Consider a time when you felt that your bones clung to your flesh. What was it like to be physically and/or mentally weary? When you felt that way, to what or whom did you turn?

Prayer: *Creator God, remind us that though we are flesh and bone, we are also spiritual beings, created for a greater purpose and calling that extends beyond physical limitations. Amen.*

Exasperation Yields Expertise

Ecclesiastes 1:18

For in much wisdom is much vexation,
and those who increase knowledge increase sorrow.

Today, we are halfway through our Lenten journey. We have faced spiritual droughts, taken inventory of our parched lives, and explored sacrifice and spiritual practice. In many ways, Lent is exhausting. It certainly was for Christ, who was called to the wilderness by the Holy Spirit and accepted that it was necessary for his ministry. But even as Jesus grew in wisdom during those forty days, he was likely annoyed, irritated, sad, and confused. We don't have a detailed gospel account of his inner dialogue, but we know that in Jesus' humanity, he must have felt distressed.

It's difficult to attain wisdom without first having had a challenge. When we think of someone who can command a stage, sport, instrument, art, or skill, we imagine it took a lot of sweat, practice, frustration, and time to get there. Experience, knowledge, and wisdom cannot arrive without sacrifice and sorrow. Lent is a refiner's fire—it's fertile training ground for a spiritual Olympics. And we are halfway through. Has there been pain and discomfort in these weeks? Perhaps. Has there been thoughtful reflection? Definitely. Either way, scripture and Christ teach us that we cannot arrive to the gifts of the wilderness without walking through deserted places.

Spiritual Practice: Take a few minutes to reflect on the first half of your Lenten experience. Return to your one-minute journal entry for Ash Wednesday when you made a list of all that you dreaded about Lent. What unexpected lessons have you learned this year? What fruit has come of any and all wrestling you've experienced to date?

Prayer: *Sustainer God, in your grace, you have equipped us for even the hardest journeys. We give you thanks for this Lenten season and the wisdom that comes from sitting with our sorrow. Amen.*

In It Together

2 Corinthians 1:7

Our hope for you is unshaken; for we know that as you share in our suffodferings, so also you share in our consolation.

There is comfort in communal suffering and sacrifice. It sounds awful to say, but humans relish the idea that we are not *completely alone* in our pain. At any given moment, there are people—family, friends, loved ones, co-workers, and even strangers—who understand our agony because they have experienced it, too. Perhaps the most powerful example this century has been the COVID-19 pandemic. Through unspeakable global loss, we connected with one another in ways that previously didn't seem possible. Across nations, neighbors helped one another; individuals made sacrifices for the greater common good, and through our suffering, we also shared in consolation.

Since COVID's arrival, we read and heard the mantra, "We are in it together." Though it's not verbatim, this is precisely what Paul meant in his letters to believers in Christ's teachings who were suffering because of their faith. For Paul, "We are in it together" would have meant that though we experience pain in this time, our comfort resides in the fact that we are not alone in our suffering and sacrifice. The Bible is timelier than we give it credit for being.

Spiritual Practice: Yesterday you returned to your Ash Wednesday one-minute journal. Please do the same today, this time examining that which made you eager for Lent. What has come from that list? Reflect on any and all goodness (including consolation) that you have received by the grace of God this liturgical season.

Prayer: *God who is our companion, we know that you share and understand our suffering. We give you thanks for this season of both dread and eagerness, because we believe that there is fruit in the path. Amen.*

Week 4: Walking through the Wilderness to Get to The Living Water

The Weary and Restless

Matthew 11:28

"Come to me, all you that are weary and are carrying heavy burdens, and I will give you rest."

We have arrived at a turning point in Lent. Three weeks in, we are entering into a time in which the living water—the spiritual gifts of the wilderness—are in sight. I often imagine Lent as a labyrinth: We enter the path exhausted, listless, and in need of recalibration. As we wind our way to the center, which is God, we begin to unpack and let go of the things from the world that we need to put down. These may be our material attachments, our ego, our craving to chase, buy, and do, as well as our aversion to turning inward. As we've walked this labyrinth-like wilderness, we've been invited to face our spiritual droughts, take inventory of our parched lives, and consider the spaces of our lives that require spiritual sacrifice.

As we approach the Center, we have a new invitation: connecting with God. Matthew's gospel reminds us that Christ invited us to "come to Him" and rest. The heavy-burdened, the lonely, the suffering, the confused, the uncertain, the angry, the bereaved, the tired—we are all invited to rest in the arms of the Center, which is God. Now that you have done the hard work of self-reflection in the first half of Lent, you are encouraged to consider what gifts lie ahead.

Spiritual Practice: Take a few minutes to return to your one-minute journal from the past several weeks. As you did the hard work of walking the wilderness labyrinth, what did you discover? Now, visualize yourself taking every burden that emerged from your writing and laying it at the center of the labyrinth. Write a few sentences about what it means to "rest" in God.

Prayer: *Triune God, we are weary. Help us to lean into Christ's calling to come and draw nearer to you, where we will find rest. Amen.*

Soul-Seekers

Lamentations 3:25

The LORD is good to those who wait for him,
to the soul that seeks him.

I forget that God needs me.

The Triune God doesn't need our material goods or money—but God does need our time and affection. It is by grace that we are in relationship with our Creator, and when we are in relationship with another being— mortal or immortal—we are called to offer our time, care, and connection. Relationships cannot grow without attention. Scripture reminds us that God is always near—we merely must seek God's presence and seek with our soul.

It's an odd feeling to think about God's *needing* us. In a way, that is what Lent is about: drudging through the grit of life to reach the gift. The gift, it turns out, is a closer relationship with our Creator, Redeemer, and Sustainer.

We may think that we don't need God and that God doesn't need us. But the Bible is clear: We were created for relationship with our Creator. The distractions of this world, like a rock in our shoe, keep us from seeking that which is eternal.

Spiritual Practice: What do you think God needs from you? Make a list. Then consider what you can offer God that transcends the things of this world.

Prayer: *Lord of all creation, we often neglect that we were created in your image and made for relationship. May our souls seek you with every breath. Amen.*

God with Us

Haggai 2:4

Take courage, all you people of the land, says the LORD; work, for I am with you, says the LORD of hosts.

One of my favorite names for God is "Emmanuel," which means "God with us." The term Emmanuel is prevalent in Advent, when we consider the incarnation of God in Jesus, but we don't often hear of Emmanuel during Lent. However, Emmanuel is not limited to one liturgical season. God is with us always—in every breath, minute, hour, and year.

As we reflect on the center of the wilderness labyrinth, preparing our hearts to walk the remainder of the desert to get to the living water, we should take courage that God is with us always.

No matter what challenges I've experienced in my own life—trauma, loss, grief, depression, anxiety, despair—I have never felt the absence of God. I realize that this, in and of itself, is a gift. Whether it's in teaspoons or a deluge of a presence, Emmanuel—God with us—has never abandoned me or you.

Spiritual Practice: List all the ways in which you recognize God's presence. There is no right or wrong answer; your relationship with God is unique to you.

Prayer: *Abiding God, help us to take courage this wilderness season, for you are with us always. Amen.*

For Sabbath's Sake

Isaiah 30:15

For thus said the Lord God, the Holy One of Israel:
In returning and rest you shall be saved;
in quietness and in trust shall be your strength.

In late 2017, I published a book called *For Sabbath's Sake.* The book was the result of my constant going and chasing—and my aversion to the inward, quiet journey of spiritual practice. Though sabbath is a core practice of Christianity, we are hesitant to rest, worship, and be in community. Various life, work, and global circumstances make embracing sacred time for quiet, trust, and humility difficult. But sabbath is a commandment, and Lent is a way of entering into a sabbath rhythm of quiet and rest.

In a 24/7 society that itches for incessant stimulation, we neglect to remember that we are people of the Book—and that book, sacred scripture, reminds us that our strength is in the quiet Center of God. As we continue to walk in the wilderness and eventually return to the world, my hope is that we remember that it is "in quietness and in trust" that we will find our strength.

Spiritual Practice: Do you embrace time for sabbath rest, worship, and community? Do you consider quiet time to be energizing or a burden? Why or why not?

Prayer: *God of Sabbath, our hearts are restless until they find rest in you. Amen.*

God Is Our Refuge

Job 30:24

*"Surely one does not turn against the needy,
when in disaster they cry for help."*

In my own life and spiritual practice, I have noticed that I often cry for help from God when I am in a disaster. In times of great distress, prayer is my go-to tool. Our God is a God of mercy and grace, a steadfast presence in times of both trouble and joy.

That said, crying for God to help is not always in my muscle memory. When we are in a distressed passage in our lives, or when we are alone in the metaphorical wilderness, recalibrating our spiritual lives may be the last thing on our minds. We may turn to shopping, doing, going, food, substance use, unhealthy habits, as well as toxic relationships and spaces. When things are stressful, it is natural and normal for humans to reach for things of this world rather than that which transcends this world.

Lent has offered us an invitation to examine our needs, our distress, and our finitude. It is also an invitation to establish spiritual practices and habits that provide us with healthy reminders to reach for God when we are in need.

Spiritual Practice: Make a list of what you turn to when you are angry, sad, stressed, lost, and needy. Examine your list and notice the spaces where you might make room to turn to God.

Prayer: *God who is our refuge and strength, help us to remember that you are a very present help in times of turmoil and trouble. Amen.*

Draw Near to God

James 4:7–8

Submit yourselves therefore to God. Resist the devil, and he will flee from you. Draw near to God, and he will draw near to you. Cleanse your hands, you sinners, and purify your hearts, you double-minded.

As mentioned before, James is one of my favorite books of the Bible. I love it for its hard-hitting, no-nonsense guidance on Christian living and reliance on God. But many preachers, teachers, and Christians bristle at James, with good reason. James's writing is not a tender softball pitch from God to us, but a tough-love letter to wake up and live into our calling.

In this passage from James, we are called to draw near to God so that God will draw near to us. Have you ever thought about your relationship with God in what way? Like two people, inching toward each other. In human terms, we take a step forward toward God, and God takes a step forward to us. James is clear that the more we move closer to the Divine, the more the Triune God will return in kind. But this biblical writer also offers conditions: clean hands, purified hearts, and a focused mind.

We are in luck, because these three conditions James lays out for drawing closer to God are precisely what we have been doing in the wilderness this Lent. Through our scripture study, spiritual practice, and examination of our own lives, we have cleansed, purified, and focused our energy on the Supreme Being. In this way, we are prepared for the closeness James urges.

Spiritual Practice: Do you feel closer to God than when you began this journey on Ash Wednesday? Make a brief list of what you think has contributed to this feeling. If you feel further from God than you did more than three weeks ago, explore that, too.

Prayer: *God of mercy, as we walk the Lenten wilderness, help us to draw nearer and nearer to you. Amen.*

God Is Our Strength

Isaiah 40:29

He gives power to the faint,
and strengthens the powerless.

As we round the corner of Week 4 of Lent, I can't help but think of how much more empowered I feel than when I began on Ash Wednesday. Maybe you do, too. The entire desert experience is about stripping down that which makes us feel faint and powerless, in order to lean into the spiritual strength and power that is the gift of the wilderness.

This verse from the prophet Isaiah reminds us that the kingdom of God is upside down. In other words, in the Lord's realm, the faint have power and the powerless have strength. But this is not the way the world works. Society, systems of oppression, and greed are perpetuated in a system that keeps humans who are already caught in the opportunity gap weary and subjugated. In our Lenten journey, we are called to recognize this reality and step into an alternative.

The grittiness of self-examination includes naming the ways we participate in keeping ourselves and others weary and powerless. When we see this clearly, we are better equipped to live by kingdom of God rules.

Spiritual Practice: How does it feel to know that God gives power to the powerless and strength to the weary? How might you remind yourself of this kingdom of God paradigm, which is often the opposite of what we experience in our daily lives?

Prayer: *God of the upside-down kingdom, help us to remember that our worldly ways are not your sacred ways. Amen.*

Week 5: Living Water for Our Parched Lives

Bookends

Ecclesiastes 7:8

Better is the end of a thing than its beginning;
the patient in spirit are better than the proud in spirit.

We are entering into the final two weeks of Lent.

We have walked the wilderness labyrinth, arrived at the Center, and are beginning to wind out of the circle as changed people. As we prepare to reenter the world, we will emerge from the desert wiser. This Ecclesiastes verse reminds us that there is a beginning and end to everything—seasons, lives, journeys, paths. In everything, patience is required, and in this case, the end is part of the reward. What the writer means to say is that the conclusion of a path is better than the start, because along the way we have grown.

In these remaining two weeks, we will examine the living water that is promised to us. We will discover the gifts of the spiritual wilderness that come from traveling through the sandy grit of self-reflection in a very loud world. In all things, patience with the process is better than pride.

Spiritual Practice: Consider beginnings and endings. Nearly every human and spiritual path has bookends; reflect on how you have changed on this Lenten journey. Make a brief list of what you've noticed.

Prayer: *Ever-Wise and Loving God, may we recognize the growth and progress we've made this Lent—not in a prideful way but, rather, in a way that makes us grateful for the process. Amen.*

Failure to Rest

Hebrews 4:1–13

Therefore, while the promise of entering his rest is still open, let us take care that none of you should seem to have failed to reach it. (v. 1)

You've probably heard the term "failure to launch." This popular English saying has application in many settings: space shuttles and adolescent children, projects and inventions. While launches of all kinds rely on a literal or metaphorical combustion that provides a boost of energy, spiritual movement and progress is just the opposite.

There is nothing we need to buy, do, or achieve to enjoy living water for our parched lives. Rather, it's what we do *not* do that produces results. Living water—the eternal well of love and abundant grace and peace provided by the Triune God—is not dependent upon earthly progress. Rather, the gifts of the spiritual wilderness rely on slowing down, resting, and turning inward. In this way, we are quiet enough to hear and experience the presence of God.

Spiritual Practice: Make a gentle list of the ways in which you fail to be still. Be kind. Do not self-punish. Rather, seek to become aware of the spaces and times where you may be more open to the invitation to rest.

Prayer: *God of rest, nudge us into the realization that failure to rest is harder on our body, mind, and soul than failure to launch. Amen.*

Delight in God

Psalm 40:8

*"I delight to do your will, O my God;
your law is within my heart."*

Have you ever delighted in God's will? Often we consider God's will to be biblical drudgery, not delight. Maybe we were raised to believe that there are rules and commandments to be followed and consequences for breaking them, and we allowed this to define God and God's will for us.

But delight should evoke joy and connection. Consider the delight you feel when you laugh with a lifelong friend or eat ice cream on a scorching July afternoon. Do you have the same experience as you ponder scripture and God's will for your life? Perhaps, or perhaps not.

The psalmist encourages us to take a view of delightedness toward God's ways. We often associate our greatest bliss with experiences and things that are of this world. But the wilderness is a place of reminders: We are finite; our lives are limited; and the more we can reach for what is eternal, the more we will experience delight that can only come from God.

Spiritual Practice: Make a list with two columns. In one, write down the people, places, and things that delight you. In the other, write down what delights you about your relationship with God. Reflect on each column. How might you lean into the latter? What would it take for you to find joy in keeping God's law (and thus God's will) in your heart?

Prayer: *Holy God, teach us to find joy in your teachings and your will for our lives. Amen.*

Our Ways Are Not God's Ways

Job 42:1–6

"Therefore I have uttered what I did not understand,
things too wonderful for me, which I did not know." (v. 3)

In many ways, I consider this verse to be one of the most important pieces of scripture for being human. These are Job's words, uttered nearly at the end of his own wilderness journey of testing in which he has suffered tremendously: loss, grief, physical ailments, abandonment, loneliness. Finally, after a conversation with God, Job begins to "understand" the crux of human suffering: We cannot, in our finite mind, understand suffering.

The point of this verse, the entire book of Job, and in many ways Lent, is that we *cannot* fully comprehend why bad things happen. Though we attempt to connect dots and make sense of suffering, it's impossible to clearly understand it with our finite human minds. And God is quick to tell Job this. Our calling, it seems, is to instead make an effort to assign meaning to our suffering.

In a method that many of us might consider unfair, God tells Job that Job is *not* the Creator, Maintainer, and Sustainer of the Universe, and therefore, Job is not capable of imagining the complexities of why humans suffer. This is a tough pill for us to swallow, but an essential one. Though Job doesn't receive the formula for why humans experience pain, he does receive comfort: living water for his literally and physically parched life, scarred by tremendous grief and testing. In the midst of it all, God never abandons Job. The same is true with us. Our ability to continue to deepen our relationship with God in times of bounty and drought help us living a more meaningful, faithful life.

Spiritual Practice: Circle back to the problem of suffering in your one-minute journal. Review your writing exercises from Weeks 1, 2, and 3. Examine the ways in which you have struggled spiritually, suffered, and made sacrifices. Now read them in light of this verse. How does reading them through the lens of Job shift your perspective, if at all?

Prayer: *God, you are all-knowing and we are not. Help us to be humble and trust. Amen.*

Two Ears and One Mouth

James 1:19

You must understand this, my beloved: let everyone be quick to listen, slow to speak, slow to anger.

There's an ancient mathematical formula that has been passed along for centuries: We have two ears and one mouth for a reason. Humans would benefit greatly if we did twice as much listening as talking. This is true for both our relationships with one another and our relationship with God. So often, we are too busy speaking, reacting, and raging to consider what others (and God) are saying to us. Why do we do this?

Perhaps it is human nature to feel that we must have the answers. In the critical thinking courses I teach to college freshman and sophomores, I urge them to consider that saying "I don't know" is a sign of a critical thinker. But perhaps we believe that by admitting we don't know, we are viewed as weak, dumb, or a coward. But that is not what the Bible teaches us.

The need to be quick to speak can be rooted in ego and culture. Instead, we are reminded that listening, thinking deeply, and responding slowly are hallmarks of virtue. It takes more effort, patience, and character to admit that we are uncertain or that we do not have a fancy answer or clever comeback. This transfers to our prayer life, too. When we pray, we should not attempt to be a know-it-all. God knows all; we do not need to prove to God that we are smart or that we have all the answers. We don't. Instead, we are invited to listen more and speak less.

Spiritual Practice: Are you a good listener? Are you slow to speak? Are you slow to answer? After five weeks of self-reflection in the Lenten wilderness, what have you discovered about yourself, and what "living water" wisdom does this verse hold for you?

Prayer: *God who teaches us to be patient and wise, help us to see the many gifts of listening for you and others. Amen.*

Living Water

John 4:7–15

Jesus answered her, "If you knew the gift of God, and who it is that is saying to you, 'Give me a drink,' you would have asked him, and he would have given you living water." (v. 10)

The story of the woman at the well is a timeless testament to finding God's presence in unlikely and unexpected places. Like her, we hardly expect to meet the Divine in a parched place, looking for water but also offering living water.

So often, God is right before us: in the face of our neighbor, a stranger, enemies, loved ones—and we don't even see it. If we did, what would we do? The Samaritan woman at the well offers us guidance. When Jesus speaks with her about "living water," she asks him where he gets it, as he has no bucket and the well is deep. She is firm, asking him if he believes himself to be greater than Jacob, who gave her and her ancestors the well for them to drink from and give to their flocks in perpetuity. But Christ is clear about the kind of water he is talking about. He tells her that the water from his man-made well will not quench human thirst. Instead, the water he is offering is a "spring of water gushing up to eternal life." The woman immediately understands the difference and asks for his "living water," that she may never thirst nor return to this well again.

The hope of Lent is that we do begin to *see and ask,* "What's the difference," just as the Samaritan woman did. The effect of the deserted, dry journey is that we have let go of that which we think we can't live without in order to reach for a "glass" of that which sustains us far beyond our physical needs. In this way, the wilderness becomes a place not of lacking, but of abundance.

Spiritual Practice: Consider all the ways in which you "meet" God in an ordinary day. Are you quick to see the sacred in what could be considered the mundane? If not, how might you be more open to it?

Prayer: *God of living water, you have given us the gift of abundant life. We merely have to see it, believe it, and ask for it. Amen.*

Walk the Talk

James 1:22–24

But be doers of the word, and not merely hearers who deceive themselves. For if any are hearers of the word and not doers, they are like those who look at themselves in a mirror; for they look at themselves and, on going away, immediately forget what they were like.

We have all been guilty of reading scripture but failing to internalize it such that it becomes a part of our lives and actions. James, in his distinct tone, doesn't mince words for those who hear the texts but do not act on them. In this way, James is not inviting us to become frenetic doers of the scriptures; rather, James is inviting us into a space of authenticity.

The wilderness is such a place. Lent is a time for rest, but not necessarily resting on our laurels. In other words, we are resting in God's will and law, so that we may emerge from Lent as changed people who are ready to accept the gifts we have been given and to share them with others.

Spiritual Practice: Make a list of the ways in which you wish to walk the talk of Christian life. Circle three that you consider your top priority. What can you do to be a doer of the word and not merely a hearer?

Prayer: *Triune God, you have given us the gift of scripture that both nourishes and calls to action. Help us to drink living water and share it with others. Amen.*

Week 6:
Holy Week

Great Is God's Faithfulness

Luke 19:28–40

"Blessed is the king
who comes in the name of the Lord!
Peace in heaven,
and glory in the highest heaven." (v. 38)

This week, we begin to emerge from the desert to reenter the world and Holy Week. Just as Jesus entered Jerusalem on Palm Sunday, it is time for us to re-turn outward to practice, share, and embody the rewards of spiritual wilderness that we have gleaned this season.

Keeping the Palm Sunday gospel narrative in mind, identify and reflect on your feelings (good and/or not-so-good) about reentry. Consider how this Palm Sunday reentry into Jerusalem would have felt to Jesus. Imagine his internal dialogue as He rode in a "king" to greet a crowd who had high hopes and expectations for his "reign." Consider how his quiet wilderness experience of sacrifice three years prior to this parade stands in sharp contrast to Palm Sunday. Reflect on how Christ's time in the desert prepared him up for this moment, which he knows will be followed by betrayal, arrest, and death. Consider how your wilderness experience prepares you for your own reentry.

In this way, we'll begin to utilize this week's reflection time to unpack the questions and themes we began with in Week 1. Now we view them through a lens of having traveled the often-gritty, hard-work path of the inward journey, knowing that God's love, mercy, and faithfulness never cease. Each morning is an opportunity to embrace the spiritual rewards we've been given.

Reflect on these questions, adapted from Week 1:

- This Lent, what did you discover about spiritual "drought"? In what ways does it impact your everyday life?
- How did noticing the drought make for a more meaningful Lent experience?

Spiritual Practice: In light of your nearly six-week journey, jot down a few bullet point answers from the two reflection questions above. Feel free to return to Week 1 to reread your one-minute journal entries on drought.

Prayer: *God who is our ever-present stream of love, mercy, and faithfulness—you bring living water to the thirsty and heal our spiritual droughts. Help us to remember to refill our wells consistently by turning inward toward you, our Center. Amen.*

Fruit for the Journey

Galatians 5:22–23

By contrast, the fruit of the Spirit is love, joy, peace, patience, kindness, generosity, faithfulness, gentleness, and self-control. There is no law against such things.

God's "inventory" is full of life-giving fruit. But so often, we focus on that which is rotten, bitter, and unhealthy for our minds, bodies, and spirits. The gifts of the spiritual wilderness include a renewed interest and craving for that which is good.

Reflect on these questions, adapted from Week 2:
- This Lent, what did you discover about taking inventory of your "parched" life?
- How did the assessment of what's abundant as well as what's lacking impact you? How did your inventory make for a more meaningful Lent experience?

Spiritual Practice: In light of your desert path, jot down a few bullet point answers from the two reflection questions above. Feel free to return to Week 2 to reread your one-minute journal entries on spiritual inventory.

Prayer: *God of abundant fruit, help us to see the goodness that has been set before us. Amen.*

Many Gifts, One Lord

1 Corinthians 12:1–11

Now there are varieties of gifts, but the same Spirit; and there are varieties of services, but the same Lord; and there are varieties of activities, but it is the same God who activates all of them in everyone. (vv. 4–6)

God has given us many gifts. But in order to receive and use them, it takes focus. Tuning out the world of materials gifts in order to tune in to our spiritual gifts takes sacrifice and spiritual practice. Lent is the ultimate training ground for discerning and sharing our gifts.

Reflect on these questions, adapted from Week 3:

- This Lent, what did you discover about sacrifice and spiritual practice?
- How did your assessment impact the way you view making sacrifices in order to share your gifts, energy, and the fruit of your spiritual practice well? How did facing the reality of sacrifice, suffering, and practice make for a more meaningful Lent experience?

Spiritual Practice: The wilderness is a place of sacrifice. In light of this, jot down a few bullet point answers from the two reflection questions above. Feel free to return to Week 3 to reread your one-minute journal entries on sacrifice and spiritual practice.

Prayer: *Holy One, you have called us to sacrifice and service. Help us to lean into ongoing spiritual practice to know your will and ways. Amen.*

By God's Grace

Ephesian 2:1–10

For by grace you have been saved through faith, and this is not your own doing; it is the gift of God—not the result of works, so that no one may boast. (vv. 8–9)

Lent is not about showing off but showing *up.* Day after day, you have showed up, receiving the gift of grace—not because of your own doing, but because of God's abundance. But recalibrating toward God takes work—not the kind of work the world favors, but the sacred work of quiet, solitude, prayer, meditation, and humility. This holy work requires grace that God gives freely and abundantly to us, Lent after Lent.

Reflect on these questions, adapted from Week 4:

- This Lent, what did you discover about what it means to do the work of walking in the *spiritual* wilderness in order to get to the living water?
- How did and does it feel to shift your focus from the external (works) to the internal (spiritual practice) in order to humble yourself and know that God's grace is a gift? How did this shift make for a more meaningful Lent experience?

Spiritual Practice: God's grace cannot be earned; it is a merciful gift. In light of your Lenten labyrinth path, jot down a few bullet point answers from the two reflection questions above. Feel free to return to Week 4 to reread your one-minute journal entries on walking through the grit to get to this very gift.

Prayer: *God of grace, help us to be humble and trust, to understand and be grateful, for you have given us the gift of abundant mercy. Amen.*

Maundy Thursday Gifts

Matthew 26:17–30

While they were eating, Jesus took a loaf of bread, and after blessing it he broke it, gave it to the disciples, and said, "Take, eat; this is my body." Then he took a cup, and after giving thanks he gave it to them, saying, "Drink from it, all of you; for this is my blood of the covenant, which is poured out for many for the forgiveness of sins." (vv. 26–28)

The cup of Christ can symbolize many things. Among them, the gift of living water—the eternal, infinite love and compassion that the Triune God extends to us through the incarnation in Jesus. We are all urged to drink from it—so that we can have abundant life.

Reflect on these questions, adapted from Week 5:

- This Lent, what "living water" did you discover? In light of Christ's offer of the cup of the covenant to his disciples, what does it mean to you to humbly receive the cup of grace extended to you?
- How does the reminder to drink from this kind of cup make for a more meaningful Lent experience?

Spiritual Practice: In light of what can feel like a vast, dry, wilderness road, jot down a few bullet point answers from the two reflection questions above. Feel free to return to Week 5 to reread your one-minute journal entries on living water for our parched lives.

Prayer: *Triune God, you have given of yourself in bread and cup. Help us never to forget this gift of plentiful spiritual food and water. Amen.*

Good Friday

Mark 15:33–40

Then Jesus gave a loud cry and breathed his last. And the curtain of the temple was torn in two, from top to bottom. Now when the centurion, who stood facing him, saw that in this way he breathed his last, he said, "Truly this man was God's Son!" (vv. 37–39)

We have walked in the Lenten wilderness according to Christ's example. We have followed the teachings of Jesus and taken his ministry into our hearts. We have recalibrated toward God, who is our Center. We have traveled the path of the Lenten labyrinth. We now return to the world and face Good Friday.

How has the wilderness prepared us for this day? How did it prepare Jesus for this day? When we consider Christ's spiritual practice and connection with God, we understand the centurion's response: "Truly this man was God's son!"

We are children of God, too. Jesus, in his humanity *and* divinity, was our exemplar. Christ demonstrated to us how to travel through the spiritual wilderness in order to glean and share its many gifts. When we look to Christ, we see humility, trust, and sacrifice. May it be so with us, too.

Spiritual Practice: As you reflect on this somber day, make a list of what Christ's Good Friday sacrifice means to you. How is Jesus an example for your own life?

Prayer: *Triune God, you have given us many gifts, but the greatest of all is in Christ Jesus. Help us to consistently look to his example, today and always. Amen.*

Holy Saturday

Luke 23:53–56

On the sabbath they rested according to the commandment. (v. 56)

While this passage is focused on Jesus's burial, the theme of rest is consistently expressed throughout this scripture passage. In this way, we are reminded that Holy Saturday is an "in-between" time for deep reflection, solitude, and *feeling* the impact of the "already and not yet."

This can also be a listless space for humans. We are eager to rush through Good Friday pain and Holy Saturday waiting. But Lent is entirely about the fruit that comes from the process. Walking the wilderness for wilderness' sake is difficult but necessary, and this, too, is part of the wilderness. We may have the (Easter) goal in mind, but let us never neglect to rest in the moment of where we are now and where we have been.

Spiritual Practice: Embrace time for rest today. In such an outcome-driven culture, write down what it means to be in the process. List all your feelings and thoughts; sit with them, just as Joseph and Jesus' friends sat with the heaviness of his burial and observed God's commandment to rest.

Prayer: *God of the Sabbath, we are reluctant to embrace the already and not yet. We are people of goals and outcomes, not process. Help us to remember that spiritual practice is a journey, not a destination. Amen.*

He Is Risen

Mark 16:1–8

But he said to them, "Do not be alarmed; you are looking for Jesus of Nazareth, who was crucified. He has been raised; he is not here. Look, there is the place they laid him. But go, tell his disciples and Peter that he is going ahead of you to Galilee; there you will see him, just as he told you." So they went out and fled from the tomb, for terror and amazement had seized them; and they said nothing to anyone, for they were afraid. (vv. 6–8)

Confusion. Fear. Perplexity. Elation. Joy. We can only imagine what the women (Mary Magdalene, Mother Mary, and Salome) felt when they saw that Jesus's body had disappeared from the tomb and learned that he had been raised. It was an urgent discovery: an unexpected gift of resurrection amid death. In many ways, Easter mirrors what we find to be true in Lent: Life *grows* in surprising places. Like our journey, we experience *gifts* where there seem none to be found: nourishment in the desert, life in the burial tomb.

After six weeks of wilderness wandering, we have arrived here with the women, astonished at the miracles God pulls off. Where there was heartache, we find joy; where there was sorrow, excitement. Lent, for all its struggles, bears much fruit: gifts of wonder and wisdom that live in perpetuity.

Spiritual Practice: Return to the "Dear Reader" section of this book. Review the answers you listed or pondered as you read these questions.

- What does Jesus's biblical retreat into solitude, sacrifice, and spiritual practice teach us about the gifts of our modern wilderness experience?
- How might a spiritual drought actually create a more meaningful Lent experience?
- What do fasting, sacrifice, and temptation look like in our contemporary daily lives?
- How might we prepare our bodies, minds, and spirits to experience new life—and gifts—on the other side of this Lenten journey?

Next, make a list of all the surprising, unexpected gifts of the spiritual wilderness you received this Lent.

Prayer: *God who astonishes us all, thank you for Easter miracles and resurrection joy. May we remember to welcome new life in unexpected places. Amen.*

Go and Tell

Luke 24:10

Now it was Mary Magdalene, Joanna, Mary the mother of James, and the other women with them who told this to the apostles.

We have only received the gospel because the women brought it to us. We have only received the gospel because Christ lived and taught it. We have only received the gospel because Jesus entered into the wilderness. Consider the abundance of fruit that has come to us from a seemingly deserted, fruit-less space. On Ash Wednesday, we exchanged drudgery for eager expectation, and gifts were bountiful.

We remember that we are no strangers to times of spiritual drought, grit, loss, stress, violence, grief, injustice, oppression, and unrest. But we are also children of God, the beneficiaries of a faith, spirituality, and a text that teaches us how to navigate our own twenty-first century wilderness experiences. This Lent, we discerned the unlikely benefits of our discomfort. Through daily devotions with scripture, meditations, practices, prayers, and "living water" tools for our parched lives, we traveled a contemplative and transformational journey where the gifts of the spiritual wilderness were boundless.

As Chalice Press and I encourage you—beseech you—go and tell. Embody and share lessons that bear fruit all year long. Continue your path of studying, journaling, praying, and sitting with the Triune God. Embrace discomfort and surprises along the way, remembering how Christ taught us that deserted places lead to Easter communion.

Spiritual Practice: Return full circle to your Ash Wednesday one-minute journal. Review the intentional statement of what you wanted to glean from Lent. What did you discover during this holy season? What gifts of the spiritual wilderness will remain with you? How will you "go and tell" to share these many gifts and encourage others?

Prayer: *God of Easter news, embolden us to go and tell of your miracles, mercies, and love. Equip us with energy to share the gifts of the spiritual wilderness, so that the hopeless will be hopeful, and the downtrodden will be encouraged. In your Holy Name, Amen.*